MANY HAPPY RETURNS

4/10

Written by Brian Enting
Photographed by Brian Enting
Additional photography by **Greenpeace Photo Library:** (children picking up garbage, cover; man sorting cans, pages 22-23; pollution from paper mill, page 35);
Photobank Image Library: (rusting car frame, page 4; girls with recycling bins, page 19; iron ore mine, page 23; glass-recycling truck, page 31); **Comstock:** (truck at landfill, page 13; boys carrying recyclable items, page 17; colored bottles, pages 32-33);
Waste Care Management: (new landfill, page 13; man testing landfill site, page 15);
Hulton Deutsch: man stacking tires, giant paper basket, page 7); **Fotopacific:** milkman and customer, page 6); **Austral International:** FPG (monitor lizard, page 27) Joseph McNally (boy with vermicomposting bin, page 43)
Illustrated by Brent Chambers

04 03 02 01 00
12 11 10 9 8 7 6

Published by Shortland Publications Inc.

Distributed in the United States of America by

Rigby

a division of Reed Elsevier Inc.
500 Coventry Lane
Crystal Lake, IL 60014
800-822-8661

Printed through Bookbuilders, Hong Kong.

ISBN: 0-7901-1005-9

MANY HAPPY RETURNS

A REVIEW OF RECYCLING

CONTENTS

INTRODUCTION

All living things create waste. Trees shed leaves, and many plants produce more flowers and fruit than they need.

Everything in nature is part of a continuous cycle of death, decay, new life, and growth. Natural waste, such as dead plants and animals, is broken down by decomposers, such as maggots, worms, bacteria, and fungi. The chemicals and nutrients they contain are then absorbed back into the soil. This acts as fertilizer, enriching the soil and stimulating new plant growth.

Nature is very efficient at dealing with waste, recycling materials again and again.

There is, however, a major difference between the "litter" created by nature, and the garbage produced by humans. Earth's natural cycles can break down some of the waste created by people. But many of these products, such as glass, tin, and some plastics, are not as biodegradable (capable of being broken down by bacteria) as "natural" packaging, such as banana skins. In many cases, nonbiodegradable wastes need human intervention to assist their return to the ground.

RECYCLING IN THE PAST

Recycling has been a part of society for centuries, and people have been reusing or selling other people's discards for thousands of years. In the Bronze Age, for example, people made things from metals and recycled them when they broke.

People were encouraged to conserve and recycle materials during World War II, as most resources were put toward the war effort. Trading systems could not operate during these times either.

Milk being delivered to the door used to be a thing of the past. However, it is now making a comeback in some cities.

Even fifty years ago, recycling was a natural way of life. Materials and resources were not as accessible as they are today, and people found a second use for many things. Most goods came wrapped in brown paper and string. The invention of modern "conveniences," such as disposable goods and plastic packaging, changed this.

ORLD'S LARGEST
E PAPER BASKET
LIT!

7

THROWAWAY SOCIETY

The Throwaway Society: it's a term invented in the late 20th century to describe the era in which we live – a time when people are using and disposing of many more items than ever before.

Some countries use more of the earth's resources than others. So-called "consumer societies," such as European countries, the United States, Canada, Japan, Australia, and New Zealand, are generally very wasteful. People in these countries are surrounded by gadgets, such as televisions, refrigerators, and computers – few of which can be recycled.

The huge amount of waste that people throw away is overloading the system, and may take many years to break down. Waste materials which are dumped and do not decompose quickly may cause pollution.

Many products of the consumer society, such as cars, have "built-in obsolescence" – that is, the make or model is not made to last and will be out of date in only a few years.

EACH YEAR, THE AVERAGE PERSON IN THE SO-CALLED "DEVELOPED WORLD" THROWS AWAY:

160 CANS

TWO TREES' WORTH OF PAPER AND CARDBOARD

107 BOTTLES

99 lb. OF PLASTIC

WHY RECYCLE?

Recycling is the process of recovering material from the home, business, or industry so that it can be reused. This process has many benefits for the throwaway society. Recycling:

• helps conserve natural resources
• helps reduce the environmental damage that may result from producing goods and disposing of waste materials
• saves energy since, in most cases, recycling requires less energy than making products from raw materials
• saves landfill space so that land can be used for other purposes
• can lead to job creation in collection schemes, recycling workshops, and stores selling recycled goods and materials

To change to a "conserver society," people need to start viewing most waste as simply material that has ended up in the wrong place.

The process of turning raw materials into manufactured goods uses large quantities of energy and exhausts precious fossil fuels. Recycling lessens the impact of industry on the environment.

Although the throwaway society still flourishes, new recycling industries are emerging, generating employment and boosting energy efficiency.

GARBAGE, GARBAGE EVERYWHERE

How big is the world's garbage problem? Most of our waste is dumped into landfills. The world's largest landfill site is near New York City. It holds an estimated 2.4 billion cubic feet of garbage – 25 times the volume of one of the great Egyptian pyramids at Giza – and it's getting bigger! New Yorkers throw out more garbage per day than anyone else in the world – 4 lb. per person.

The most basic landfills are little more than large holes in the ground where garbage is left to decompose. Without direct sunlight, the decaying process takes place very slowly.

Normally, garbage biodegrades when it's in contact with the right amount of air and water. By sealing it off from air or moisture, many landfills have actually been preserving garbage.

Garbage used to be dumped on top of unoccupied land, but these days, it may be buried underground.

Many older landfills create environmental problems, such as the leaching of toxins from the garbage into groundwater, which causes water pollution.

Modern landfills contain leachate in specially lined cells. On-site water is channeled into ponds, which are monitored.

GARBOLOGISTS AT WORK

Garbologists are scientists who study garbage. By studying landfills, they understand the composition and long-term fate of tons of buried debris.

The most up-to-date landfills dump waste into specially prepared cells, which are covered over daily. Better still are those landfills which have recycling plants attached. Reusing garbage is an excellent way of reducing the problems of waste disposal. More companies worldwide are recycling glass, paper, metal, and plastic.

In many countries, active landfills are reaching their capacity. As the number of operating landfills shrinks, scientists need to know what we're throwing out so they can make decisions about how to manage this garbage in the future.

14

Modern landfills employ a number of people to monitor different aspects of their operations. Samples of groundwater are regularly collected from wells around the site and tested.

Some students from the University of Arizona examine garbage as part of an archeological study. The study's aim is to understand the eating and waste disposal trends of city-dwelling people from various economic backgrounds so that future waste management plans can be worked out.

RECYCLING BEGINS AT HOME

The first step in a good recycling program is to reduce the amount of garbage brought into the house in the first place. Use the three R's as a guideline:

- REDUCE as much waste as possible
- REUSE items for other purposes or give them to other people
- RECYCLE items so that resources can be used again

Choosing goods which have minimal packaging, and recyclable glass rather than plastic containers are other ways to reduce waste. Be inventive in your recycling. Give unwanted things or outgrown clothes to charities. Consider also buying secondhand clothes from thrift stores, rather than getting new clothing all the time.

Avoid unnecessary packaging and refuse extra bags used in stores – take your own shopping bag or reuse old tote bags instead. If you still need bags from stores, paper bags are a better choice than plastic ones. Try not to buy disposable things.

RECYCLING BEGINS AT HOME CONTINUED

In many towns, garbage is grouped into different batches and collected for recycling. Recycling centers for sorted garbage are located in many neighborhoods. Ask your local chamber of commerce for information about recycling collection points in your area – bottle, can, and paper recycling centers – and what their plans are for introducing more.

Garbage should be divided up as soon as it has been used, and then placed in containers for different types of waste. These could include:

- PAPER for recycling, preferably folded flat
- ALUMINUM CANS for recycling
- OTHER CANS for recycling (wash them and crush flat)
- GLASS for recycling (wash and remove labels)
- PLASTICS that can be recycled (check to see if there's a recycling symbol on the container)
- FOOD SCRAPS and organic material for composting
- NONRECYCLABLES, such as certain plastics, for the garbage can

Recycling will ensure that the kitchen garbage can shrinks in size!

CLEAR

BROWN
GLASS

RECYCLE GLASS THROUGH THE
BOTTLE BANK
AND SUPPORT YOUR COMMUNITY

PLASTIC
ONLY PLEASE

19

MAKING A COMPOST PILE

WHAT YOU NEED:
- compost bin
- lime fertilizer
- soil
- garden refuse
- kitchen scraps
- worms (optional)

WHAT TO DO:
1. Mix the waste with a little soil or some existing compost.
2. Build the compost with alternate layers of wet and dry waste.
3. Sprinkle some lime on top of each layer as it is added to the heap.
4. Turn the compost over regularly with a pitchfork. It should be ready to use after several months, or when it looks like dark, crumbly, sweet-smelling soil.

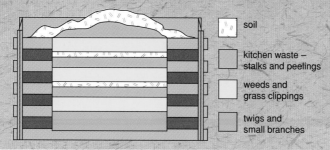

- soil
- kitchen waste – stalks and peelings
- weeds and grass clippings
- twigs and small branches

YOU CAN USE:
- food scraps
- fruit
- vegetables
- peelings
- tea leaves/bags
- coffee grounds
- paper
- blood and bone fertilizer
- old flowers
- lawn clippings
- weeds
- leaves
- vacuum cleaner dust
- fireplace ashes
- small rags
- animal manure

DON'T USE:
- plastic
- fats
- large bones
- oily or waxy materials

20

Hay is used to insulate a compost pile and help moderate its temperature.

Compost creates new organic matter, which is the lifeblood of the garden. Adding compost fixes poor soils which are lacking nutrients. This, in turn, helps many types of plants to grow.

METAL MELTDOWN

We use many different products made of metal in our everyday lives. Some types of food, especially drinks, are packaged in metal containers.

Cans are made of either tin or aluminum, or a mixture of both. Both of these are expensive metals, and the mining of them is often destructive to the environment. Mining strips the soil and can lead to erosion.

Most cans can be recycled. In the case of aluminum, reusing scrap metal requires 95 percent less energy than making new cans.

Unfortunately, some containers are made of mixed metal, which can't be recycled. Cans made of a mixture of alloys need to be separated for recycling. Containers can be easily tested with a magnet – aluminum is not magnetic.

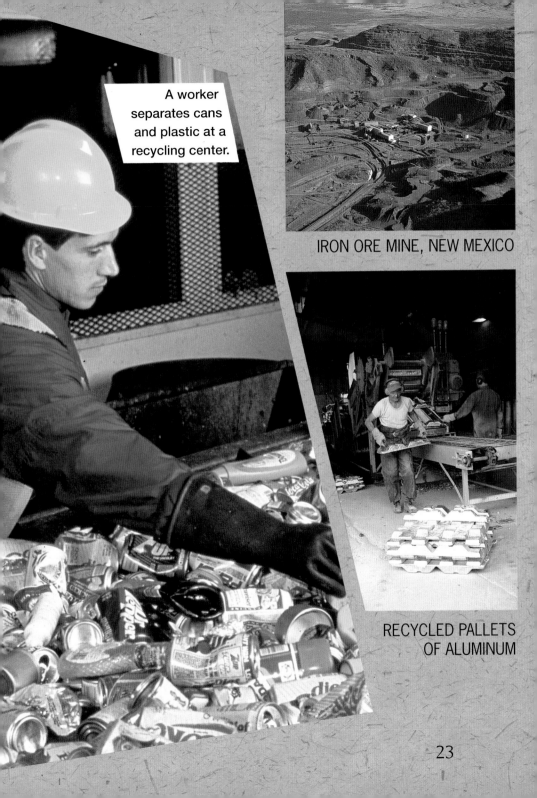

A worker separates cans and plastic at a recycling center.

IRON ORE MINE, NEW MEXICO

RECYCLED PALLETS OF ALUMINUM

RECYCLING CANS

This is what happens after you put a can into a recycling bin:

1 At the furnace, the cans are combined with scrap aluminum and pressed into solid bales for easy handling.

4 The molten metal is then poured into molds to produce ingots: solid bars of aluminum. These are used to produce a wide range of finished goods, such as soft drink cans and aluminum car hubcaps.

2 The scrap metal is placed in a large, rotating kiln and heated until the aluminum has melted completely.

3 This liquid is poured into a holding tank where chemicals can be added to produce different aluminum alloys.

25

NOT-SO-FANTASTIC PLASTIC

Waste plastic takes a very long time to break down in the soil. Some plastics are thought to take 400 years to biodegrade in the ocean! That's why after a beach cleanup, there's always more plastic than anything else in the trash bags.

Scientists have invented two new types of plastic, biodegradable and photodegradable, which break down at a faster pace. Both types, however, disintegrate into a fine plastic dust, which itself causes pollution. Also, biodegradable plastic won't break down in dry conditions, and photodegradable plastic needs direct sunlight to break down.

Plastic is a hazard to marine life. Birds and other animals are sometimes strangled by plastic strapping. Whales and turtles can choke on plastic bags, which they mistake for jellyfish.

RECYCLING PLASTIC

There are hundreds of different types of plastic in the world, used for a great many things. This diversity can cause problems when it comes to recycling. At present, only seven of the most common types of plastic are recycled internationally. A name or number coding system on the packaging indicates which plastic it is. Soft drink bottles, for example, have the symbol with a "1," while milk containers have a "2." Each type of plastic is collected and recycled separately.

⚠1 PET – polyethylene terephthalate

⚠2 HDPE – high-density polyethylene

⚠3 PVC – polyvinyl chloride

⚠4 LDPE – low-density polyethylene

⚠5 PP – polypropylene

⚠6 PS – polystyrene

⚠7 OTHER – all other resins and
          layered multi-material

Different types of waste plastic are sorted according to their various melting points.

2 The plastic is shredded and washed in water.

In this pliable form, the plastic is forced into different molds to make plant pots, pipes, and buckets. Recycled plastic is not used for food products, as it is difficult to clean completely.

3 Once the plastic is dry, a machine called an agglomerator spins and turns the shredded plastic into tiny crumbs. These are fed into a machine and heated until they melt into a solid mass.

BROKEN GLASS

Unlike plastic, glass packaging can be hygienically cleaned, and either refilled or recycled. This saves raw materials, as well as the energy used in manufacturing new glass.

Refilling glass uses even less energy than recycling. A glass milk bottle, for example, can be reused 100 times, unlike plastic containers or cardboard cartons, which are one-way packaging only.

Deposit systems encourage more people to recycle glass. These projects increase the price of bottled products, but the money is paid back to customers when they return bottles to the store.

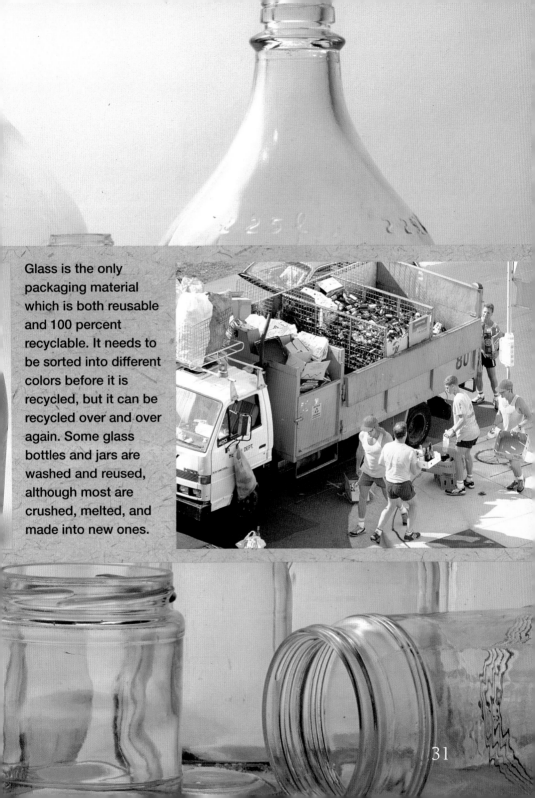

Glass is the only packaging material which is both reusable and 100 percent recyclable. It needs to be sorted into different colors before it is recycled, but it can be recycled over and over again. Some glass bottles and jars are washed and reused, although most are crushed, melted, and made into new ones.

RECYCLING GLASS

1 After it's been collected, the glass is sorted into different colors.

4 The recycled "recipe" is heated in a furnace until it melts. This mixture is then shaped in a mold that determines the shape of the glass – in this case, bottles.

2 The glass is then cleaned and any labels are removed. Next, the glass is ground into small chips, which are called *cullet*.

3 Glass manufacturing usually requires high levels of energy to melt the mixture of sand, soda, ash, limestone, and silica. Making recycled glass uses about 15 percent less energy than producing brand-new glass, as cullet melts at a lower temperature.

GLASS ONLY

THE PAPER CAPER

The Computer Age was supposed to make us a paperless society. But we are in more danger than ever of disappearing under a mountain of paper. Paper products make up the largest percentage of waste from both industry and homes.

Seventeen trees, or nearly a quarter of an acre (0.1 hectares) of forest, are needed to make one ton of paper.

There is growing concern about the quantity of trees being cut down for paper and wood products. The vast South American rain forest, which acts as the "lungs" of our planet, is being milled rapidly. The trees breathe in carbon dioxide, and release oxygen, the gas we need to breathe.

The process of turning wood pulp into paper consumes large quantities of energy, exhausting precious fossil fuel resources. Making recycled paper uses half as much energy as new paper production and reduces water and air pollution.

PULP AND PAPER OUTFLOW INTO THE RIO TINTO, HUELVA, SPAIN

RECYCLING PAPER

1 The wastepaper is first shredded and made into bales.

4 Finally, the pulp turns back into paper, which is stored on large rolls. Packaging materials, such as cardboard and egg cartons, are made from recycled paper, and many items like writing paper are now 100 percent recycled.

2 A front-end loader moves the bales of wastepaper to the conveyor belt, which carries them into a machine called a hydrapulper. This acts like a giant kitchen blender, mixing the wastepaper with hot water at high speed until the paper fibers break down into a pulpy mass.

3 The pulp is cleaned to remove unwanted matter, like paper clips and glue. It is then diluted to a mixture which is 99 percent water, and chemicals are added to strengthen the paper. This watery mess is sprayed onto a large moving belt and enters the pulp-drying machine, which removes all the water.

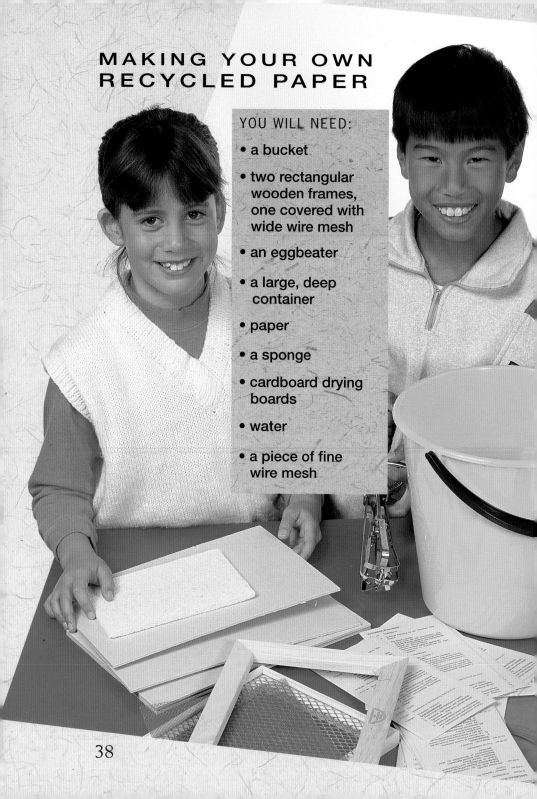

MAKING YOUR OWN RECYCLED PAPER

YOU WILL NEED:

- a bucket
- two rectangular wooden frames, one covered with wide wire mesh
- an eggbeater
- a large, deep container
- paper
- a sponge
- cardboard drying boards
- water
- a piece of fine wire mesh

1 Rip the paper into postage-stamp-size pieces. Tear up about five cupfuls. Put into a bucket and completely cover with hot water. Soak for at least fifteen minutes, or overnight, if possible.

2 Use the eggbeater to beat the paper into a pulp. Pour the pulp into the large container and add about 4 inches of water. Stir the mixture.

MAKING YOUR OWN
RECYCLED PAPER
CONTINUED

3 Place the fine wire mesh on top of the wide mesh frame. Use the empty wooden frames to make a "paper sandwich." Dip this into the pulp mixture.

6 Place the sponge on top of the mesh and gently press down to remove excess water. Peel the fine mesh off the paper. Leave the new sheet of paper until it is completely dry, then peel it off the drying board.

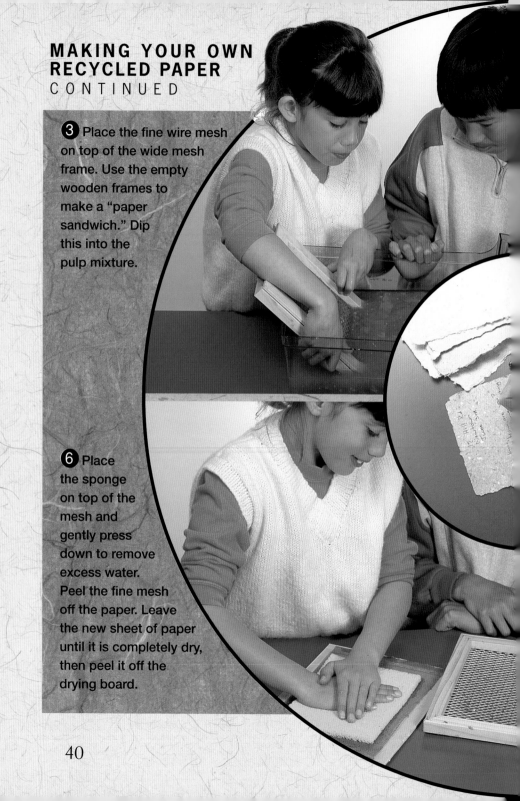

40

4 Lift up the frames covered with a thin, even layer of pulp over the mesh. Drain off the water.

5 Remove the top frame. Place a drying board on top of the fine mesh. Carefully turn everything over so that the frame is on top of the drying board. Remove the other wooden frame.

41

ECO-KIDS

Many children all over the world are involved in recycling projects and are aware of the impact that recycling can make on their environment. If recycling begins at home, it can continue at school and in the community. Eco-kids take part in projects like beach cleanups, paper-making, trashless lunches, energy and water conservation... even composting with worms! Earth Day is April 22 every year, but eco-kids make every day an Earth Day.

WORM BINS

Vermicomposting is the process in which worms recycle organic waste. Forty-five pounds of worms can change forty-five pounds of waste into soil in one month! Earthworms tunnel through the ground, making places for water and air to enter, and aerating soil by turning it over. They drag leaves and other bits of food down into the soil, which decay, making soil more fertile.

- red worms – smaller species, available from most pet shops

- some good, rich garden soil

- worm food, such as leafy vegetable bits, grass cuttings, carrot and potato peelings, and coffee grounds

43

THE RECYCLING GAME

Here's how you can make learning about recycling fun...
Create your own recycling board game!
All you will need are:

- *two dice*   • *counters*   • *colored markers*
- *a sheet of heavy cardboard for the board game*
- *sheets of lighter cardboard for the quiz cards*

The aim of the game is to be the first to get from the beginning to the end of the path. Draw the background setting onto the board so that it looks like a neighborhood with houses, stores, parks, schools, etc., then write instructions on selected squares. These directions should all be linked to recycling, with players rewarded for doing something good (e.g., taking cans to a recycling center, go forward 2 squares), or penalized for doing something bad (e.g., littering, miss a turn).

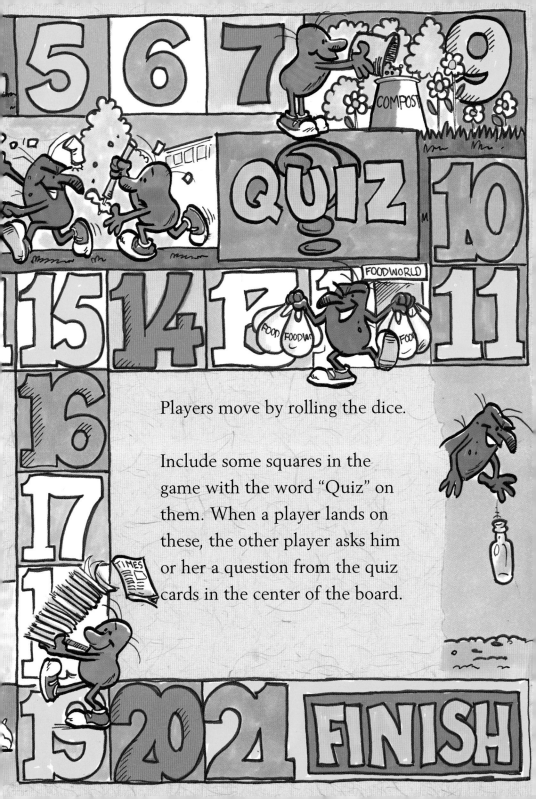

Players move by rolling the dice.

Include some squares in the game with the word "Quiz" on them. When a player lands on these, the other player asks him or her a question from the quiz cards in the center of the board.

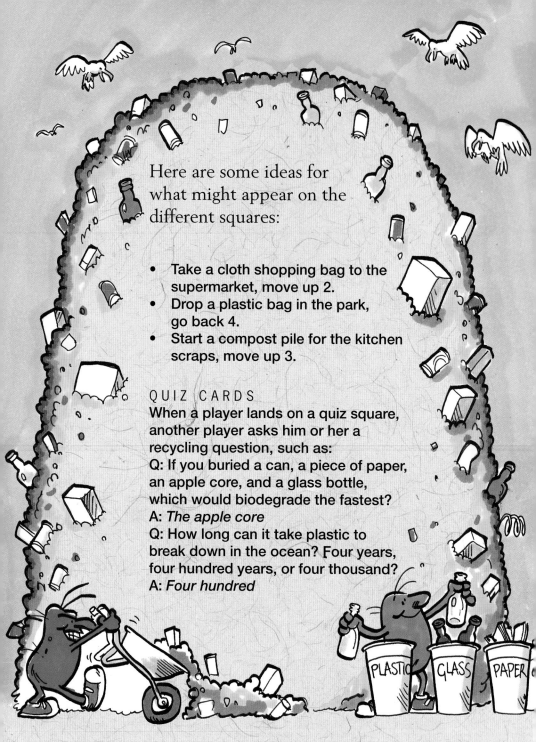

Here are some ideas for what might appear on the different squares:

- Take a cloth shopping bag to the supermarket, move up 2.
- Drop a plastic bag in the park, go back 4.
- Start a compost pile for the kitchen scraps, move up 3.

QUIZ CARDS

When a player lands on a quiz square, another player asks him or her a recycling question, such as:

Q: If you buried a can, a piece of paper, an apple core, and a glass bottle, which would biodegrade the fastest?
A: *The apple core*

Q: How long can it take plastic to break down in the ocean? Four years, four hundred years, or four thousand?
A: *Four hundred*

PLASTIC   GLASS   PAPER

GLOSSARY

agglomerator – a machine that collects fragments, such as plastic, and bonds them under heat

aluminum – a light, silvery metal which is easily molded

biodegradable – a substance that can be broken down by the natural processes of decomposition

compost – a nutrient-rich mixture of ingredients, usually made from layers of kitchen waste, grass clippings, and leaves

consumer society – the name given to communities where many people "consume," or buy, many things

cullet – recycled broken glass, which is used to make new glass

decomposer – something that breaks down dead material, such as bacteria or worms, putting nutrients back into the environment

fertilizer – a substance that enables plants to grow

garbage – something that has been thrown away

landfill site – a place where solid waste is disposed of, usually a hole in the ground

nonbiodegradable – a substance that can't be broken down in the environment

nonrecyclable – an item that can't be recycled

photodegradable – describes an object that can be broken down by the sun's rays

recycling – the processing of waste products for reuse

vermicomposting – the process of using worms to make compost

waste – something left over, or not used

TITLES IN THE SERIES

SET 9A

Television Drama
Time for Sale
The Shady Deal
The Loch Ness Monster Mystery
Secrets of the Desert

SET 9B

To JJ From CC
Pandora's Box
The Birthday Disaster
The Song of the Mantis
Helping the Hoiho

SET 9C

Glumly
Rupert and the Griffin
The Tree, the Trunk, and the Tuba
Errol the Peril
Cassidy's Magic

SET 9D

Barney
Get a Grip, Pip!
Casey's Case
Dear Future
Strange Meetings

SET 10A

A Battle of Words
The Rainbow Solution
Fortune's Friend
Eureka
It's a Frog's Life

SET 10B

The Cat Burglar of Pethaven Drive
The Matchbox
In Search of the Great Bears
Many Happy Returns
Spider Relatives

SET 10C

Horrible Hank
Brian's Brilliant Career
Fernitickles
It's All in Your Mind,
    James Robert
Wing High, Gooftah

SET 10D

The Week of the Jellyhoppers
Timothy Whuffenpuffen-
    Whippersnapper
Timedetectors
Ryan's Dog Ringo
The Secret of Kiribu Tapu Lagoon